21st CENTURY LIVES
BOLLYWOOD STARS

Liz Gogerly

WAYLAND

First published in 2010 by Wayland

Copyright © Wayland 2010

Wayland
338 Euston Road
London NW1 3BH

Wayland Australia
Level 17/207 Kent Street
Sydney, NSW 2000

Editor: Julia Adams
Designer: Rebecca Painter
Picture researcher: Shelley Noronha

Picture Acknowledgments:
p1 Rex Features (repeat pg 10); p4 PIYAL ADHIKARY/epa/Corbis; p5 Rex Features; p6 Rex Features;
p7 Excel Entertainment/The Kobal Collection; p8 DAMFX/The Kobal Collection;
p9 Rex Features; p10 Rex Features (repeat pg 1); p11 Dharma Productions/The Kobal Collection;
p12 Hubert Boesl/dpa/Corbis; p13 Sean Gallup/Getty Images; p14 Colin McPherson/Corbis;
p15 Yash Raj Films/The Kobal Collection; p16 STR/epa/Corbis; p17 Rex Features; p18 Toussaint
Kluiters/Reuters/Corbis; Cover & p19 Dharma Productions/The Kobal Collection; p20 PUNIT
PARANJPE/Reuters/Corbis; p21 Rex Features;

British Library Cataloguing in Publication Data:
Gogerly, Liz.
    Bollywood stars. -- (21st century lives)
    1. Motion picture actors and actresses--India--
Biography--Juvenile literature.
I. Title II. Series
791.4'3'028'0922'54-dc22

Printed in China

ISBN: 978 0 7502 6206 4

Wayland is a division of Hachette Children's Books, an Hachette UK company

www.hachette.co.uk

Contents

Rani Mukerji
The Adventurous Actress

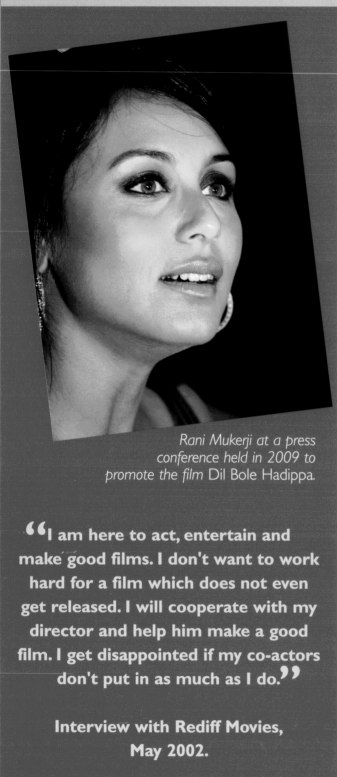

Rani Mukerji at a press conference held in 2009 to promote the film Dil Bole Hadippa.

"I am here to act, entertain and make good films. I don't want to work hard for a film which does not even get released. I will cooperate with my director and help him make a good film. I get disappointed if my co-actors don't put in as much as I do."

Interview with Rediff Movies, May 2002.

Real name: Rani Mukerji (she changed the English translation of her name from Mukherjee to Mukerji).

Date and place of birth: 21 March 1978, Calcutta, West Bengal, India.

Background: Film-making is in Rani's blood. Her father Ram Mukherjee is a director and helped to found the Filmalaya Studios. Her brother Raja is a producer and director. Her cousin Kajol is a famous Bollywood actress and her aunt Debashree Roy was a Bengali film actress.

Famous Films: Rani's big break was in 1998 when she co-starred in the romantic drama *Kuch Kuch Hota Hai (Something Happens)*. The film was the highest-grossing Indian movie of the year and launched Rani into the Bollywood limelight. Rani has appeared in nearly 50 movies, not all of them such hits. Her most critically acclaimed appearances are in *Chalte Chalte* (2003), *Yuva* (2004), *Hum Tum* (2004), *Veer-Zaara* (2004), *Black* (2005), *Bunty Aur Babli* (2005), *Kabhi Alvida naa Kehna* (2006), *Laaga Chunari Mein Daag* (2007) and *Saawariya* (2007).

Most memorable movie moment: Playing the part of a deaf-blind girl in the 2004 hit *Black*.

Awards or achievements: Rani became the first actress to scoop two Filmfare awards in 2004. She won Best Actress award for *Hum Tum* and Best Supporting Actress for *Yuva*.

Something you might not know about her: Before Rani became a household name she appeared in ads for Lux Soap and Fanta Orange Drink.

Rani Mukerji and Saif Ali Khan melted hearts in the 2004 smash hit *Hum Tum*. The duo have worked their magic in many more collaborations.

Rani was born into one of India's leading film families. However, the Bollywood star claims that she never set out to become an actor. While she was at college in Mumbai she was offered film work, but she turned it down. At this time Rani was slightly overweight and not an obvious star. Family friend and film producer Salim Akhtar must have seen her potential. He convinced her to star in *Raja Ki Aayegi Baraat* (1997). In the film Rani played a rape victim. She received good reviews but the film flopped. Rani returned to college for a while, but in 1998 she was back on the silver screen. Her part in the love story *Ghulam* turned her into a household name. Later that year she accepted a part in *Kuch Kuch Hota Hai*. The film went on to become the biggest Bollywood smash of the year and Rani received her first Filmfare Award for Best Supporting Actress.

Rani isn't afraid to take on varied and challenging screen roles. In 2001 she accepted the lead in the ground-breaking *Chori Chori Chupke Chupke*, the first Bollywood movie about surrogate childbirth. In 2003 she took on her first comic role in *Chalte Chalte*. Then in 2004 she starred alongside Saif Ali Khan in the thoroughly modern romantic comedy *Hum Tum*. Rani earned her first Filmfare Award for Best Actress. In 2005 Rani stunned audiences with her performance as deaf–blind girl Michelle McNally. Rani spent six months at the Helen Keller Institute in Mumbai preparing for the role. Critics called it her best performance to date.

Rani ranks as one of Bollywood's finest actresses but in recent years she has taken on less work to spend more time with her family. In 2009 she played a female cricketer in the film *Dil Bole Hadippa*. Famous for her curves, audiences were shocked by her new slim-downed appearance. The film was not the box-office hit that people expected, leading some critics to question what Rani will do next. Rani has a simple philosophy which helps to keep her feet on the ground: "Keep smiling and spread the word of love, as it always grows!"

"It is not any bias that makes me regard Rani in a certain manner. Rani is a tremendously gifted and spontaneous actor who brings her naturalness alive on the screen."

Amitabh Bachchan

Amitabh Bachchan
King of Bollywood

Bollywood legend Amitabh Bachchan in 2007. This was the year Amitabh starred in his first English-language film The Last Lear.

"I don't use any techniques; I'm not trained to be an actor. I just enjoy working in films. It's more instinctive rather than anything else. I don't do the calculated rehearsed kind of approach, and I hope that I can continue that because I believe that instinct is much stronger and greater when you are performing on camera."

Amitabh, interview with CNN, July 2007

Real name: Amitabh Harivansh Bachchan

Date and place of birth: 11 October, 1942 Allahabad, Uttar Pradesh.

Background: Amitabh is the son of Hindi poet Dr Harivansh Rai Bachchan. His mother Teji loved theatre and persuaded her son to act.

Famous Films:
Amitabh has made well over one hundred movies, so it's impossible to list all the famous films. In the 1970s Amitabh became a mega star with parts in *Deewar* and *Sholay,* considered by many critics to be amongst the best Bollywood movies of all time. Other 1970s hits include *Amar Akbar Anthony, Kabhi Kabhi* and *Don.* Later successes include *Coolie* (1983), *Shahenshah* (1988), *Agneepath* (1990), *Mohabbatein* (2000), *Black* (2005), *Sarkar* (2005) *Cheeni Kum* (2007), *The Last Lear* (2007) and *Paa* (2009)

Most Memorable Movie Moment:
Many critics would say Amitabh's moving performance in the movie *Black* is his finest acting.

Awards or achievements: Amitabh has won all the major Indian film and entertainment awards including Filmfare awards, Star Screen Awards and Stardust Awards. He has been nominated for the Filmfare Award for Best Actor 29 times, which is the record.

Something you might not know about him: In 2000 he became the first living Asian to be cast in wax and displayed at London's Madame Tussauds wax museum.

Amitabh Bachchan has been called 'Bollywood's Shahenshah [King of Kings]' and the 'one man industry'. Famous for his deep baritone voice and dark brooding looks, he has also been described as a cross between Clint Eastwood, Al Pacino and Elvis Presley with a hint of John Travolta. Amitabh has been part of the Indian film industry for over forty years. In that time he has acted, sung and danced his way into fans' hearts. He is versatile and creative and has played the villain, the lover, the comedian, the tragic hero and the action hero.

Amitabh attended the University of Delhi where he studied for a Bachelor of Science degree. After college came a job in freight broking, but Amitabh was eager to become an actor. In 1969 he made his film debut in *Saat Hindustani*, a performance for which he received a National Film Award for New Comer. However, it was a few years before the tall, lanky actor would make it big time. The breakthrough came in the 1973 classic action move *Zanjeer*. Amitabh's fighting spirit wrapped up in his dark brooding looks meant he became known as the 'angry young man' of Bollywood.

The 1970s were golden years for Amitabh's acting career. Then, in the early 1980s, he nearly lost his life when filming *Coolie*. Afterwards Amitabh took a break from acting to try politics. He served as a Member of Parliament from 1983 to 1987. His movie comeback in 1988 was the smash hit *Shahenshah*. Success was short-lived and many critics believed his acting days were over. Amitabh proved the critics wrong with his 2000 performance in *Mohabbatein* for which he won a Filmfare award. The same year Amitabh became the face of Kaun Banega Crorepati, the Indian version of the quiz show *Who Wants to Be a Millionaire?*.

Amitabh has continued to shine on the big screen throughout the 2000s. In 2007 he made his first English language film *The Last Lear*. Now in his sixties Amitabh shows little sign of slowing down: "I'd like to believe that tomorrow is another challenge for me. I'm sure there is lots more for me to do, because there is lots and lots of stuff still to be explored".

Amitabh in the 2004 Bollywood film *Lakshya*. He starred alongside upcoming actors Hrithik Roshan and Preity Zinta in the story based on the 1999 Kargil Conflict.

"If you are not going to compare me to him (Amitabh), whom are you going to compare me to? I have never had a problem being compared to him and, like I said, who doesn't want to be compared to Amitabh Bachchan? He is the best we have and the best that we ever will have. It's a matter of great honour for me."

Abhishek Bachchan, *Indiatimes Movies* January 2010.

Aishwarya Rai
Beauty Queen of Bollywood

Aishwarya Rai radiated beauty in the 2002 film Devdas. At time of filming, it was the most expensive film ever made in Bollywood.

"My biggest award is when people stand up and appreciate me. Not only audiences, but also directors, seniors and co-stars who recognise my worth. And I always wanted to carve the niche for myself, to be recognised as an actress. Name, fame, glamour, fan following were all there. The awards are icing on the cake."

http://www.aishwaryaforever.info/ aishwarya-interviews/aishwarya-rai-a-personal-interview.html

Real name: Aishwarya Rai Bachchan

Date and place of birth: 1 November 1973, Mangalore, Karnataka, India.

Background: Ash (her name is often shortened to Ash or Aish) was a bright student studying for a career in architecture when she was crowned Miss World in 1994.

Famous Films: Ash's first role was in the Tamil movie *Iruvar* in 1997. She became a Bollywood star with the release of *Hum Dil De Chuke Sanam* in 1999. Other Bollywood box office hits include *Devdas* (2002) and *Dhoom 2* (2006). Hollywood movies include *Bride & Prejudice* (2004) and *The Pink Panther 2* (2009).

Most Memorable Movie Moment: Playing a young woman torn between her husband and her first love in *Hum Dil De Chuke Sanam*. This is considered her breakthrough performance.

Awards or achievements: Ash has won two Filmfare Awards for Best Actress. She won the award for the part of Nandini in *Hum Dil De Chuke Sanam* in 2000. She scooped a second award in 2002 for her moving portrayal of Paro in the blockbuster *Devdas*.

Something you might not know about her: In 2005 the toy manufacturer Mattel made a limited-edition Barbie doll inspired by Aishwarya and her costumes. The dolls sold out quickly and are now very collectable.

East meets West in the 2004 Indian/English/American film *Bride and Prejudice*. Based on the novel *Pride and Prejudice* by Jane Austen, the film introduced many Western viewers to Aishwarya Rai (front row, yellow sari).

Ash is arguably the most famous Indian actress of all time. Already a star in her native India, she moves in international circles and acts in Hollywood movies. With her mesmerising blue-green eyes she is also considered to be the most beautiful woman in the world. In India she is a style icon and stars in cosmetic giant L'Oreal's advertisements all round the globe.

Ash grew up in a strict middle-class home in Mumbai. Her father was a merchant marine and was often away working. Ash was a serious student with an interest in zoology and biology. However, she was studying to become an architect when she first tried out modelling. In 1994 she entered the Miss India contest and went on to win Miss World. Ash stood out for her warmth and intelligence. She wanted to change the way people in the world thought about India.

Ash can speak four Indian languages, as well as English. She made her film debut in the Tamil film *Iruvar* in 1997. The following year she scored another commercial hit in another Tamil movie, *Jeans*. Her big Bollywood breakthrough was *Hum Dil De Chuke Sanam* in 1999. Since then she's received gushing reviews for her parts in *Josh*, *Devdas* and *Mohabbatein*. By 2004 Ash's star performances had captured the attention of movie directors overseas. Ash's part in the Bollywood-style English movie *Bride and Prejudice* introduced many Westerners to the talented young actress. The film also helped to bring Bollywood movies to a whole new audience. Ash went on to become the first Bollywood star on US programme *Oprah Winfrey*. She is rumoured to have turned down the part in *Mr and Mrs Smith* that was eventually taken by Angelina Jolie.

In 2007 Ash was welcomed into one of Bollywood's top acting families when she married fellow actor Abhishek Bachchan. That year she ventured outside Bollywood in another English film called *Provoked*. Ash picked up good reviews for her portrayal of an abused Punjabi woman living in London. In 2009 Ash starred in *The Pink Panther 2* with Steve Martin. Though the film was a flop, many critics still think Ash has what it takes to make it big in Hollywood.

"When Hollywood women are so exposed—there's something wonderful about a woman who is sensible and refined, mysterious and sensual."

Bride and Prejudice co-star Martin Henderson about Aishwarya Rai.
Time Asia, 20 October 2003

Hrithik Roshan
India's Biggest Heartthrob

Hrithik Roshan promotes the 2010 movie Kites *at the famous Cannes Film Festival in France. The Bollywood movie is set in the USA.*

"Oh, I'm never satisfied. I'm always trying to aim for more, I'm a perfectionist. Honestly, sometimes when people praise me, I want to tell them to stop it. Call me modest or whatever, I'd rather let my work speak for me."

http://hrithikroshan.tripod.com/interviews.htm

Real name: Hrithik Roshan

Date and place of birth: 10 January, 1974, Mumbai, Maharashtra, India.

Background: Hrithik grew up surrounded by film crew and actors. He made his film debut aged six and took on a few small roles as a boy. Acting didn't get in the way of his studies and he has a Bachelor of Commerce degree.

Famous Films: Hrithik was an instant star in his debut film *Kaho Naa… Pyaar Hai* in 2000. Other top movies include: *Koi… Mil Gaya* (2003), *Krrish* (2006), *Dhoom 2* (2006) and *Jodhaa Akbar* (2008)

Memorable Movie Moment: In 2008 Hrithik won the Filmfare Best Actor Award for his portrayal of Akbar the Great in the historic love epic *Jodhaa Akbar*. Hrithik was every bit the Emperor in the war scenes and a passionate lover in the shots he shared with Aishwarya Rai.

Awards or achievements: Since 2000 he has won many best actor awards, but winning the Filmfare awards for Male Debut and Best Actor in 2000 for *Kaho Naa… Pyaar Hai* was a stunning start to his career.

Something you might not know about him: He had a dreadful stammer as a boy. The problem was so bad that he could hardly make himself understood. For many years he had to do special exercises every day. He recently opened a speech therapy school to help other people with the same problem.

Hrithik-mania hit India in 2000 when the young actor took on his first lead role in the film *Kaho Naa… Pyaar Hai*. In many ways Hrithik was primed to become a Bollywood star, but nobody, including himself, expected such an overwhelming reaction.

Hrithik was born into a film family. His father Rakesh Roshan is a famous film director. His mother Pinky is the daughter of the producer and director J. Om Prakash. Hrithik always wanted to be an actor and he had small parts in his father's films while he was a child. However, he admits that directing films is his first love and something he will return to when he is older. His career in films began when he worked as assistant director to his father. Rather than hobnob with the stars, Hrithik worked hard with the rest of the film crew. Now that Hrithik is one of Bollywood's greatest actors, but he still likes to get involved in helping the set run smoothly.

Hrithik was his father's assistant for five years. In 2000 he thought he would be helping his father to direct *Kaho Naa… Pyaar Hai*. He kept asking his father which Bollywood superstar he was going to cast as the lead. It came as a surprise when his father turned round and said: "You're the hero of my film." Hrithik wanted to be perfect for his debut role. He immediately joined acting, dancing and martial arts classes. The hard work paid off with *Kaho Naa… Pyaar Hai* becoming the Bollywood hit of the year and Hrithik scooping two Filmfare awards.

With his light-green eyes, a dazzling smile and rippling muscles Hrithik is one of the new generation of Bollywood actors. He impressed audiences with the lead role in the science fiction film *Koi… Mil Gaya* in 2003. His return to the super hero role in the sequel *Krrish* in 2006 earned him more awards and recognition. The same year he starred in the action move *Dhoom 2*. In 2008 he scooped his first international award for Best Actor for his multi-award winning performance in the historic epic *Jodhaa Akbar* . For a while, there were rumours that he would be the next James Bond. At the moment Hrithik remains Bollywood's golden boy, but one day Hollywood may beckon.

"I will always try to have him in all my future projects because he is a complete actor. If you give him any kind of role, he will rise to the challenge and shoulder the responsibility to the T…"

Film director and producer Rakesh Roshan, *South Asia Focus*, June 2009

Shahrukh Khan
King Khan

It's a winner! Shahrukh Khan promotes the 2007 Chak De India, the film in which he plays the coach of the Indian woman's hockey team.

"Even if I were a corporate type, I'd be an actor. If I was a major in the army and was dying in a battlefield, my death would be as heroic as those death scenes in the movies. I was born only to act. You can take me out of the actor, but you can't take the actor out of me."

http://www.seasonsindia.com/
cinemascope/iviewShahrukh
1_sea.htm

Real name: Shahrukh Khan, although he prefers to be called Shah Rukh.

Date and place of birth: 2 November 1965, New Delhi, India.

Background: Shahrukh grew up watching films at the cinema. At school he was good at drama and he gained a Bachelors degree in Economics at college. He began studying towards a Masters Degree in Mass Communications but dropped out to train as an actor at Delhi's Theatre Action Group. He made his television debut in 1988.

Famous films: He won the Filmfare Best Male Debut Award for his part in the 1992 film *Deewana*. He scooped Filmfare awards for *Baazigar* (1993), *Kabhi Haan Kabhi Naa* (1993), *Anjaam* (1994), *Dilwale Dulhania Le Jayenge* (1995), *Dil To Pagal Hai* (1997), *Kuch Kuch Hota Hai* (1998), *Mohabbatein* (2000), *Devdas* (2002), *Swades* (2004) and *Chak De India* (2007).

Memorable Movie Moment: Shahrukh's favourite role was playing a musician in the 1993 film *Kabhi Hann Kabhi Naa*.

Awards or achievements: In 2008 the magazine *Newsweek* claimed Shahrukh to be one of the 50 most powerful people in the world.

Something you might not know about him: He has vowed that he will never do a proper kiss on screen.

The Bollywood actor, producer and quiz show host *Shahrukh Khan* has been called the King of Bollywood. He's been the action hero and the villain, but now he's most famous for playing the lover in feel-good movies.

Shahrukh was born in New Delhi to Muslim parents. His father ran a transport company and his mother was a magistrate and social worker. At school Shahrukh was a star pupil, but his mother had to push him to study Hindi with the promise of trips to the cinema. Shahrukh loved the cinema, but he wanted to get into making television commercials. After university he studied towards making commercials, but the drive to become an actor soon took over. In the 1980s he made a name for himself on television, starring in soaps. The most famous was the soap *Circus,* which hit the screens in 1989.

Shahrukh Khan signs autographs for German fans at the premiere of *Om Shanti Om* in Berlin (2008).

Shahrukh's parents died in 1991 and he made the decision to move to Mumbai. The same year he married his childhood sweetheart Gauri Chibber. He had no intention of becoming a Bollywood actor, but claims that he needed the money to support his family. The next year he made his Bollywood debut in the hit movie *Deewana.* He admits that receiving the Filmfare award that year was the most special moment of his career. Shahrukh went on to become one of the top Bollywood stars of the decade with leads in all-time classics *Dilwale Dulhania Le Jayenge* and *Kuch Kuch Hota Hai.*

Shahrukh stayed on top of the game throughout the 2000s. Some of his critics think that his performances have become predictable, but the Bollywood giant has starred in a string of box office winners, including *Mohabbatein, Devdas, Chalte Chalte, Main Hoon Na, Veer-Zaara, Swades, Chak De India* and *Om Shanti Om.* Shahrukh has also set up his own production companies, *Dreamz Unlimited* and *Red Chillies Entertainment.* In 2007, Shahrukh was back on television screens. This time he replaced screen legend Amitabh Bachchan as the new host of the quiz show *Kaun Banega Crorepati* [the Indian version of *Who Wants to be a Millionaire?*].

"For me, Robert DeNiro is the yardstick for acting. So are Dustin Hoffman and Tom Cruise. Arnold Schwarzenegger is the yardstick for success. I may never reach those heights, realistically speaking. I may never even achieve the kind of success Shammi Kapoor, Amitabh Bachchan, Rajesh Khanna and Sanjeev Kumar did. But I will always keep on trying."

http://www.sharukhkhan.info/sharukh-interviews/shahrukh-getting-emotional-.-an-interview.html

Preity Zinta
Happy-go-lucky Heroine

Preity Zinta charms her fans as she pulls up on the red carpet at the 2007 International Indian Film Academy Awards (IIFA). These awards are also known as the 'Bollywood Oscars'.

"Basically, I see myself as a representative of the 21st century. I'm not going to do films which project women as relegated to the kitchen or as objects of desire. Our films are the archival material which portray what this century is about and, so, I want to do progressive films."

http://www.rediff.com/movies/2000/may/22preity.htm

Real name: Preity Zinta

Date and place of birth: 31 January 1975, Shimla, Himachal Pradesh, India.

Background: Preity was a good student and gained an English Honours degree and a postgraduate degree in criminal psychology. She went onto become a model and progressed into film.

Famous Films: Preity first hit the big screen in 1998 in *Dil Se* and *Soldier*, both of which she received Filmfare awards. Critically acclaimed performances in *Kya Kehna* (2000) and *Chori Chori Chupke Chupke* (2001) ensured her reputation as one of Bollywood's most exciting new actresses. Awards for *Armaan* (2003) and *Kal Ho Naa Ho* (2003) followed. She's also remembered for her parts in *Veer-Zaara* (2004), *Salaam Namaste* (2005), *Kabhi Alvida Naa Kehna* (2006) and *The Last Lear* (2007)

Memorable Movie Moments: Preity's first movie release was the 1998 film *Dil Se*. Though she was only in the film for 20 minutes, she wowed audience with her performance as Shahrukh Khan's feisty fiancée.

Awards or achievements: Though Preity has won Filmfare Awards for Best Actress in her native India, she has also won the award for Best Actress (Silver Hugo) at the Chicago International Festival for her part in the Canadian film *Heaven on Earth (2008)*.

Something you might not know about her: In 2009 Preity left Bollywood to study at Harvard Business School in the USA. The actress was taking a course in negotiating and deal making.

Preity Zinta plays a star-crossed lover in the 2004 blockbuster *Veer-Zaara*.

Preity Zinta is one of Bollywood's most charismatic stars. Known for her open smile and easy-going attitude, she is very popular with audiences and the film industry. Behind that famous grin and dimple there is a brave actress who likes to throw herself into varied roles. So much so, she has been credited with changing the idea of the classic Hindi film heroine.

Preity was born into a military family. Her father was strict and Preity and her two brothers were very disciplined. Tragedy struck early in her life when her father was killed and her mother was badly injured in a car accident. Preity had to help a lot at home, but she did well at school and college. Later, her fresh-faced good looks meant she was picked out to work as a model. She first caught the public eye in an advertisement for Perk chocolates and Liril soap. She was also noticed by prominent film directors and made her screen debut in *Dil Se* (1998), for which she won the Filmfare Award for Best Female Debut.

What is the secret of Preity's popularity and success? As a person Preity is forthright and not afraid to stand up for what she believes. She is well-known for being outspoken and this means standing up to directors, too. She works hard to make her characters feel real

and has changed her look and style for nearly every role she has taken. In 2000 she played a teenage single mother in *Kya Kehna*. She didn't win awards for her part the 2001 blockbuster *Dil Chahta Hai*, but she claims the film was a turning point in her career. The film had a modern feel and centred on a group of young well-off friends living in the city. In *Chori Chori Chupke Chupke* (2001) Preity took on a controversial role when she played a prostitute who agrees to become a surrogate mother.

The list of challenging roles continued, including playing a schizophrenic in *Armaan* (2003), the romantic lead in the love story *Veer-Zaara* (2004) and the sophisticated fashion editor in the popular *Kabhi Alvida Naa Kehna* (2006). More recently, Preity has broadened her horizons with parts in the art movies *The Last Lear* (2007) and *Heroes* (2008).

"I love her bluntness, her jovial nature, her positive thinking. I like her happy personality."

Salman Khan about Preity Zinta

Aamir Khan
The Perfectionist Superstar

Bollywood actor Aamir Khan has plenty to smile about as he celebrates his 44th birthday in 2009 – his latest film 3 Idiots *is the highest-grossing Bollywood film of all time.*

> "I'm very ambitious. I'd like to do work of the level people haven't seen before. I want to raise the bar as an actor, producer and director. I'd like to do films that would live on much after I'm no longer there. Even if someone sees *Lagaan* 200 years later, he should say, 'Who's that guy, yaar?'"

http://entertainment.oneindia.in/
bollywood/interviews/2009/
aamir-khan-interview-070109.html

Real name: Aamir Hussain Khan

Date and place of birth: 14 March 1965, Mumbai, Maharashtra, India.

Background: Aamir grew up around the Hindi film industry. His father was the Indian film producer Tahir Hussain. His uncle Nasir Hussain was also a film producer and actor.

Famous Films: Aamir's breakthrough came in 1988 in *Qayamat Se Qayamat Tak* when he won the Filmfare Best Male Debut Award. In the 1990s, critically acclaimed performances in *Dil Hai Ki Manta Nahin* (1991), *Jo Jeeta Wohi Sikandar* (1992), *Hum Hain Rahi Pyar Ke* (1993), *Andaz Apna Apna* (1994), *Rangeela* (1995), *Raja Hindustani* (1996), *Ghulam* (1998) and *Sarfarosh* (1999) turned him into a Bollywood great. In 2001 he produced and starred in the smash hit *Lagaan*. Performances in *Ghaini* (2008) and *3 Idiots* (2009) keep Aamir top of the league.

Most Memorable Movie Moments: Some would say his debut in *Qayamat Se Qayamat Tak* when Aamir first won audiences over with his boyish charm. Twenty years later Aamir had audiences in stitches with his comic performances in *3 Idiots*, the "highest grossing Bollywood movie of all time".

Awards or achievements: Aamir avoids the limelight and doesn't attend awards ceremonies because he feels Indian film awards are not credible. Even so, he has won and been nominated for awards many times.

Something you might not know about him: Aamir played tennis at national level when he was a teenager. He admires Swiss world champion Roger Federer.

Aamir Khan produced and played the lead in the 2001 epic saga *Lagaan*. Set during the Victorian era of the British Raj, the film was an international success.

Aamir has gone on to become one of Bollywood's most admired actors. He's well known for being choosy about his projects. Fans eagerly await each new film, because Aamir promises to bring something different to each character he plays. He's rarely backed a loser; highlights of his career include playing a rebellious villager in *Lagaan* (2001), for which he won a Filmfare Award for Best Actor. He won another Filmfare award in 2006 for his part in the action drama *Rang De Basanti*.

In 2007 he made his directional debut in *Taare Zameen Par*, in which he also played the part of an inspirational teacher to special needs children. In 2008 he went through a tough fitness programme to become an extremely muscular rich businessman with severe amnesia in *Ghajini*. Many fans say that playing a student engineer in the 2009 hit *3 Idiots* is among his best performances, least of all because he was playing a man much younger than himself. Aamir has the talent and the power to make a Hollywood film but the actor stays true to himself. Until the right script and the right director come his way, he's in Bollywood to stay.

Aamir Khan has directed one film, produced three and acted in about 40 Hindi movies. He has been called the Bollywood Sean Penn because of his 'method acting' style. A perfectionist and thoughtful actor, he never takes on more than one film at a time.

Aamir first appeared in one of his uncle's [Nasir Hussain] movies when he was a child. Aamir claims that he was chosen to be in *Yaadon Ki Baaraat* (1973), just because he was part of the family and happened to be the right age. Aamir's desire to become an actor kicked in years later when he was 16. He helped a school mate make a home movie. Aamir got involved in the whole process from directing to acting and loved it. His family was against him becoming an actor and tried to encourage him to stick at his studies. Aamir did not formally train to become an actor, but he found a job in the local film industry. His big break came when his cousin Mansoor Khan cast him in the romantic *Qayamat Se Qayamat Tak* in 1988. The handsome young lead became a teen idol with sacks of female fan mail.

"…when I actually met him I was surprised at the way he submits himself to a film project. His total involvement took me by surprise. He was so committed to the film that he would wake up in the middle of the night to get into the skin of his character. Working with Aamir Khan has made me his admirer and I would love to work with him again."

The director of *3 Idiots*, Rajkumar Hirani

Kareena Kapoor
Queen Bebo of Bollywood

Kareena Kapoor brings Bollywood glamour to the 2009 International Indian Film Academy (IIFA) awards in Amsterdam.

"**Acting is in my blood. I have that passion in me. Whatever I do, I will give my 100 per cent to it. I am of the belief that an actor should know to switch from one role to another effortlessly, like Aamir Khan and Saif do.**"

http://www.glamsham.com/movies/interviews/24-kareena-kapoor-interview-110916.asp

Real name: Kareena Kapoor

Date and place of birth: 21 September 1980, Mumbai, Maharashtra, India.

Background: Kareena is part of the famous film family, the Kapoors. Her father Randhir Kapoor, her mother Babita and her sister Karisma were all actors.

Famous films: Kareena made her debut in the 2000 film *Refugee*. Next came the internationally acclaimed *Kabhi Khushi Kabhie Gham* (2001). Kareena has gone on to star in *Chameli* (2004), *Dev* (2004), *Omkara* (2006), *Jab We Met* (2007) and *3 Idiots* (2009)

Memorable Movie Moment: In 2003, Kareena stunned her critics when she played a prostitute in *Chameli*. Her moving performance earned her a Filmfare Special Performance Award.

Awards or achievements: In her short career Kareena has won Filmfare awards for Best Performance and Best Actress. She is considered by many to be one of the most powerful actresses in Bollywood.

Something you might not know about her: She's a great cook and whips up magnificent desserts. She loves food and one and half hours of yoga each day keeps her body in shape and her mind in focus.

Lights, camera, action: Kareena Kapoor holds her own in a cast brimming with Bollywood superstars in the 2001 hit *Kabhi Khushi Kabhie Gham.*

Kareena always dreamed of becoming an actress. Since her screen debut in 2000 she has lived the dream. She has starred in blockbusting movies alongside some of Bollywood's finest actors, including Amitabh Bachchan, Abhishek Bachchan, Hrithik Roshan, Shahrukh Khan and Aamir Khan. These days she even dates one of Bollywood's best, the actor Saif Ali Khan.

Being born into a film family doesn't mean it's going to be easy getting into the film business. Kareena's father Randhir was set against Kareena and her older sister Karisma becoming actresses, believing that women should look after the family. Eventually, their mother Babita left her husband to raise her girls alone. Kareena did well at school. After school she attended college in Mumbai and studied commerce. Later, when she was studying law, she realised something fundamental about herself — she didn't want to sit behind a desk for the rest of her life; she wanted to act. A stint at acting school followed then in 2000 she was offered her first part in *Refugee*.

Kareena has starred in over 30 movies. After initial success in films like *Mujhe Kucch Kehna Hai* (2001) and *Kabhi Khushi Kabhie Gham* (2001), she starred in a few box office disasters. Worst of all, some critics said Kareena's performances were unoriginal. Kareena bounced back in the 2004 drama *Chameli* with her sensitive portrayal of a prostitute. What was the secret of Kareena's magnificent performance? Though *Chameli* was essentially a street-wise, tough girl, Kareena brought a dignity and innocence to her character that somehow made her more real. She brought the same naturalness to the Sikh girl she played in the love story *Jab We Met* in 2007. Since then she has starred in the highest grossing Bollywood film of all times, *3 Idiots* (2009). Kareena's dreams have all come true, but the feisty actress still has one more dream: "God willing, one day one of my movies will win an Oscar too."

"Kareena is outstanding, a great and instinctive actress, extremely committed, a team player, we get along well, and she's good looking... what more can one ask for?"

Aamir Khan

19

Saif Ali Khan
The Little Prince

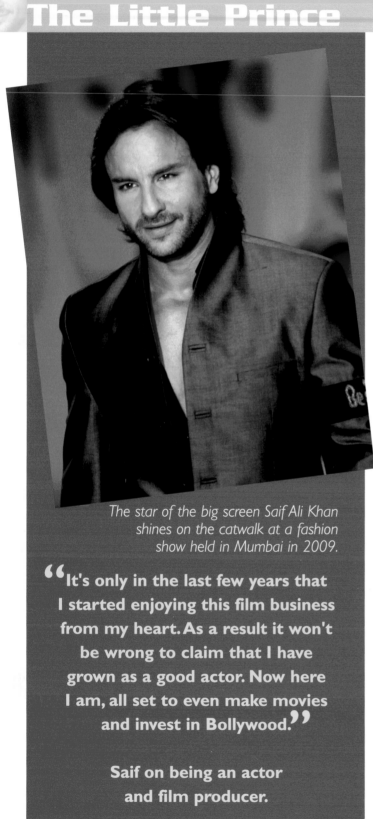

The star of the big screen Saif Ali Khan shines on the catwalk at a fashion show held in Mumbai in 2009.

"It's only in the last few years that I started enjoying this film business from my heart. As a result it won't be wrong to claim that I have grown as a good actor. Now here I am, all set to even make movies and invest in Bollywood."

Saif on being an actor and film producer.

Real name: Saif Ali Khan

Date and place of birth: 16 August 1970, New Delhi, India.

Background: Saif is the son of Mansoor Ali Khan, the Nawab [originally the title for a leader of an Indian state or a Muslim noble] of Pataudi and former captain of the Indian cricket team, and the Bengali actress Sharmila Tagore. As a child, Saif wasn't sure if he wanted to become a cricketer or an actor.

Famous Films: Saif won a Filmfare Best Male Debut for the 1993 film *Aashiq Aawara*. The following year he was praised for his parts in *Yeh Dillagi* and *Main Khiladi Tu Anari*. He made a return to the big screen in *Dil Chahta Hai* (2001) and has gone on to star in *Kal Ho Naa Ho* (2003), *Hum Tum* (2004), *Salaam Namaste* (2005), *Parineeta* (2005), *Omkara* (2006), *Race* (2008), *Kurbaan* (2009) and *Love Aaj Kal* (2009).

Most Memorable Movie Moment: In 2006 Saif stole the show in *Omkara*, the Indian language version of the Shakespeare classic *Othello*. Saif's portrayal of the treacherous Langda Tyagi (Iago in the original Shakespeare play) earned him mighty praise from the critics. One critic claimed, "It's Khan's movie through and through."

Awards or achievements: He has won the Filmfare Best Comedian Awards twice for the 2001 modern romance *Dil Chahta Hai* and the 2004 'rom com' *Hum Tum*.

Something you might not know about him: In 2009 Saif published his autobiography: *I Am Here to Stray.*

Saif Ali Khan and Rani Mukerji make a winning team in the 2004 'rom com' *Hum Tum*. The film is based on the Hollywood classic *When Harry Met Sally*.

Saif Ali Khan has had his share of Bollywood highs and lows. He's played the comedian, the romantic and the action hero and in real life he's been called a wild child. Critics applauded him in the early 1990s, but he was off the radar until 2001 when he bounced back in the blockbuster *Dil Chahta Hai*. These days the Bollywood star has a more serious reputation as an actor. He's even set up his own production company *Illuminati*.

As the only child of a cricket hero and a famous actress, Saif was perhaps destined to become a celebrity himself. He spent much of his childhood at boarding school in England, but always spent the holidays at home in Bhopal and Bombay. As a boy he often accompanied his mother on film sets. Saif's own passage onto the big screen has been a bumpy affair. His wild-child tendencies caused him to be thrown off his first movie project. In 1992 he finally made his debut in *Parampara*, but his breakthrough came in the love story *Yeh Dillagi* (1994).

Saif is the first person to admit he has had to work hard at becoming a movie star. He claims he didn't have the looks, while critics said he couldn't dance or act. A series of flops during the 1990s didn't deter him either. He never lets the box office disasters get him down for long because he doesn't think success is necessarily about talent. Since 2002 Saif's career has never looked back. Playing the lead in the comedy *Hum Tum* (2004) earned him his first Filmfare Best Actor award. He scooped a second Filmfare Best Actor award in 2008 for *Love Aaj Kal*. This film also marked his debut as a film producer.

Saif's acting and production skills mean he's guaranteed a place in Bollywood history. However, his bad boy image and his romantic life keep him in the news. In 2004 he was divorced from his long-term wife Amrita Singh. These days he has a high profile relationship with actress Kareena Kapoor. Photographs of the golden couple and rumours about a Bollywood wedding mean Saif always hits the headlines.

"Kurbaan is embellished with superlative performances. Saif is extra-ordinary in a role that only proves his versatility once again. If he won your heart with a winning performance in *Love Aaj Kal* a few months ago, you need to watch this supremely talented actor underplay his part so beautifully in *Kurbaan*."

Taran Adarsh, *Bollywood Hungama*, November 2009.

Other Bollywood Stars

Akshay Kumar

Akshay Kumar has been one of Bollywood's most prominent stars throughout the 1990s and 2000s. Akshay was born Rajiv Hari Om-Bhatia on 9 September 1967 in Amritsar, Punjab, India. His father was a government worker and always encouraged Rajiv to get into sport. After college Rajiv moved to Bangkok in Thailand and studied martial arts. Later, he lived in Mumbai and worked as a martial arts teacher. Singled out for his good looks he was soon modelling. This lead to film offers and in 1991 he made his debut in *Saugandh* – the film star Akshay Kumar was born. Akshay's breakthrough was the 1992 thriller *Khiladi*, an Indian version of James Bond. A series of *Khiladi* films followed, establishing Akshay as a top action hero. The 1994 romance *Yeh Dillagi* saw Akshay breaking out of the action hero mould. Akshay has made over 90 films, picking up awards for his comic performances (*Garam Masala*, 2005) and playing the villain (*Ajnabee*, 2001).

Kajol

With four Filmfare Awards for Best Actress, Kajol is one of Bollywood's most talented actresses. Kajol Mukherjee was born on 5 August, 1975 in Mumbai, Maharashtra, India. She is a member of one of Bollywood's most famous film families. Her mother is the actress Tanuja, her father Shomu Mukherjee was a film producer and her cousin Rani Mukerji is a top actress. Kajol's first film was the 1992 romance *Bekhudi*. In 1995 she hit the big time when she won her first Filmfare Award for her part in *Dilwale Dulhania Le Jayenge*. 1998 was a spectacular year in which she was nominated for best actress for three films, winning the award for *Kuch Kuch Hota Hai*. Subsequently, she has won the award for *Kabhi Khushi Kabhie Gham* (2001) and *Fanaa* (2006).

Shahid Kapoor

One of Bollywood's youngest talents and viewed by many as 'one to watch' is actor and dancer Shahid Kapoor. Shahid was born on 25 February 1981 in Delhi, India to actor Pankaj Kapoor and actress/dancer Neelima Azeem. He trained as a dancer and at 18 he starred in a Pepsi advert alongside Sharukh Khan, Kajol and Rani Mukerji. After a string of films as a background dancer his good looks and original performances were finally noticed. In 2003 he was picked to play the lead in the love story *Ishq Vishk*, for which he won the Filmfare Best Male Debut Award. The year 2006 was a turning point for the fresh-faced Kapoor with starring roles in the popular comedy *Chup Chup Ke* and the successful romance *Vivah*. The following year he starred in the box office hit *Jab We Met*. In 2009 Shahid played the part of two twins in the critically acclaimed crime thriller *Kaminey*.

Salman Khan

Packed full of muscles and attitude, Salmon Khan is a tough act to follow in Bollywood. The Bollywood bad boy was born Abdul Rashid Salim Salmon Khan on 27 December 1965 in Indore, Madhya Pradesh in India. His father is the famous writer Salim Khan. Salman's Bollywood debut was the 1989 smash hit *Maine Pyar Kiya*. He won the Filmfare Best Male Debut award and a crowd of female fans. The new heartthrob went on to star in *Saajan* (1991), *Hum Aapke Hain Koun* (1994), *Andaz Apna Apna* (1994), *Karan Arjun* (1995) and *Khamoshi: The Musical* (1996). In 1998 he picked up a Filmfare Award for Best Supporting Actor in *Kuch Kuch Hota Hai*. Despite nominations for Filmfare Awards for *Biwi No. 1* (1999), *Hum Dil De Chuke Sanam* (1999), *Tere Naam* (2003), *Baghban* (2003), *No Entry* (2005) the hot-headed hero is yet to scoop another Filmfare award.

Priyanka Chopra

Young, beautiful and already with Filmfare Awards for Best Female Debut, Best Actress and Best Villain to her name, Priyanka is one to watch in Bollywood. Priyanka was born on 18 July 1982 in Jamshedpur, Jharkand, India. With a father working as a doctor for the Indian Army, Priyanka was used to being uprooted to new places, including America. She attended college in Mumbai, but left when she won the 2000 Miss World (beauty competition). Her film career kicked off in 2002 with the lead in the Tamil romance *Thamizhan*. The following year Priyanka was big news in Bollywood with starring roles in *The Hero: Love Story of a Spy* and *Andaaz*, for which she won the Filmfare Award for Best Female Debut. Priyanka's career has gone from strength to strength. In 2004 she earned critical acclaim for her part as the selfish and power-crazy Sonia in *Aitraaz*. In 2008 she finally scooped the Filmfare Award for Best Actress for playing a model in the hit film *Fashion*.

Abhishek Bachchan

Following in the footsteps of his father, the screen legend Amitabh Bachchan, is no easy business, but actor Abhishek Bachchan is proving himself one of Bollywood's finest contemporary actors. Abhishek was born on 5 February 1976 in Mumbai, Maharashtra, India. In 2000 Abhishek made his debut in *Refugee*. His first major hit was the action film *Dhoom* (2004). The following year he starred in the four hit movies *Bunty Aur Babli*, *Sarkar*, *Dus* and *Bluffmaster*. In 2006 he was on top form in *Kabhi Alvida Naa Kehna* and in 2007 he stole the show in *Guru*. Abhishek was nominated for the Filmfare Best Actor award in 2008 for his comedy *Dostana*. The film was a box office success but *Abhishek* didn't win the award. With a handful of Filmfare Awards for Best Supporting Actors, it won't be long before Abhishek finally wins the best actor award. Abhishek is married to top Bollywood actress Aishwarya Rai.

Deepika Padukone

One to watch in Bollywood is the up and coming actress and super model Deepika Padukone. Deepika was born in Copenhagen, Denmark in 1986 but her family moved back home to India when she was a year old. She began modelling at 17 and became a famous face for Liril soap and Maybelline cosmetics. She made her acting debut in 2006, but her Bollywood break was the 2007 blockbuster *Om Shanti Om*. The film features over 40 Bollywood stars but it was Deepika and screen legend Shahrukh Khan who stole the show. Deepika also picked up the Filmfare Best Female Debut Award for 2007. It's early days for Deepika's acting career but she's already won critics over with performances in hits like *Love Aaj Kal* (2009) and *Housefull* (2010). Meanwhile, the young actress seems to have her feet firmly on the ground: "I have a very long way to go in terms of my acting abilities. To me failure and success are two sides of the same coin and accepting them both equally is what I truly believe shapes me as the person that I am. So all I can say is bring it on!"

Ranbir Kapoor

Another newcomer tipped for the top in Bollywood is Ranbir Kapoor. Born into one of Bollywood most famous families in 1982, Ranbir is no stranger to the acting profession. His parents Rishi Kapoor and Neetu Singh are actors. Directing, production and acting in Bollywood films goes back five generations in the Kapoor family. Ranbir made his own debut in 2007 in *Saawariya*, for which he received the Filmfare Best Male Debut Award. The year 2009 was a winning year for Ranbir with critically acclaimed performances in *Wake up Sid*, *Ajab Prem Ki Ghazab Kahani* and *Rocket Singh: Salesman of the Year*. Ranbir's good looks have already turned him into a teenage idol but the young actor is serious about his work: "I want to do some memorable roles in films. I want to work with good actors, actresses, directors and producers."

Index

21st Century Lives

Contents of books in the series:

WAYLAND